The Blue Hour

Angelina D'Roza

Longbarrow Press

Published in 2023 by
Longbarrow Press
76 Holme Lane
Sheffield
S6 4JW

www.longbarrowpress.com

Printed by T.J. Books Ltd,
Padstow, Cornwall

ISBN 978-1-906175-47-4

First edition

The Blue Hour

Contents

Credence

No more the slippery cloudlike moon.
Give us one clear morning after another

– Rumi

Correspondences

Magnolia

What was that thing you said about the two trees
how in representing nothing but themselves each is a home?
I touch one, then the other. One is distance

one displacement. Or the work of keeping a tree alive
compared with my own wild state. I ask for what I need.
A branch breaks through a pane of window.

Fairytale No. 17

Because I am no longer there, the market still stands, the way some people fill the space memory leaves with a plausible alternative. The market stairwell's where I learnt the word *loitering*. And later, on the gallery, is where I got my head shaved, after, but not because of, a miscarriage. They promised the best clementines for the best prices. I bought coconut/pineapple bubble bath that made my bathroom smell like the 'Copacabana'. I believe in the olfactory hallucinations of lovers apart, the impossibility of holding still. I buy yards of cotton in gingham and daisies, drink tea the colour of clay and climb the hill home.

I fill the space with wildflowers
a consolation of daisies.
My womb is an interlude of violets.
My tongue is a foxglove.

I have never considered how aphasia is not always only a loss of speech but is also sometimes the loss of thought. Is it enough to picture a hill, when there's so much to think about why I'm picturing this hill? I climb the hill home, past the brutalist flats that have been bought and sold with a marriage proposal, and where one of the newly renovated balconies blasts Radio Three. The soprano says, *the most famous love theme in the world has nothing to do with happiness.* If the story were lost, and I could only feel in silence or music, what would I feel? But how could I answer? How could I ask?

Self Portrait with Son

Too much to say, I say this whole hilltop was abundant with buckthorn and horses, mares trampling wiry bramble from The Pheasant to Bellhouse, to stand at the junction and wait for the Shiregreen wind to blow through them, the way spring blows through a city, and then you were born, and here we are, returned to The Horseshoe, a game of darts, the sky falling in through a derelict roof. Floorboards have begun to panic-flower harebells, little bluish groupies you gather for the table, as though you're not listening, but I know you hear it all, all these things to say about love and letting go, that it's possible to figure time in the damselfly among the glittering row of optics, that every flight the length of the bar is a day gone, a day gone, whole months counting a measure more or less of light, the way light comes to imitate moving on. You take my hand and only say have faith, and my heart is like a damselfly caught under a glass, held to the sky, its bejewelled and clamorous beating, beating

Lullaby

i.

It started with a river, the way cities do, a glitter in the grass hardly more than a cabbage-white wing, a heart flick faint as stars and as far away. *Flesh of my Flesh*, the lullaby goes. It started with birds, a hatch of sparrows, the way all small birds are sparrows, in the backyard honeysuckle. *Bone of my bone.* Let the birds and rivers name themselves. The fairy-wren teaches her offspring the song she'll know them by, stitches each note to the next, threading it out between them.

ii.

I call you grandson, and you look
and in that look, you become my grandson.

Like this, like light returning from one mirror
to another, we create each other.

Frangipani

I've been reading about motherhood
a little late, perhaps, the good-enough mother,
attachment theory, was I proximal

or distal. *If all the parts that were you*
are now me, can I be called Mother?
What I think about now is not whether

a reconditioned ship can still be
called *Argo*, but how to consider a ship
built from its discarded woodwork.

Am I discarded? The wreckage
of my body holds my grandson to my chest
to feel his quick breathing (proximal).

And then I leave, which is not distal
only distant. I land 2am local time, home
to the stray cats, the humidity,

a lark singing-in the moon-bright flowers
in love with the illusion of light.

Shore

There's the fractured circle of a date palm,
a low sea wall.
                    For language, the dhow boat
that cuts the Gulf in two, between me

and the blue morning mist. I'm learning
this flat earth, the equation of shade
            against the eloquence of distance.

*

The grass and birdsong are hard to resolve.

Who told the sand it wasn't enough,
to aspire to lushness? I aspire to lushness.

*

3am when the sand's blue, and everything's blue
so that nothing is separate or special, or all is

special, considered in blue gleams of tide
and mollusc arriving and arriving, say it. Blue.

*

I'm wild about this flat earth that sticks
to my feet, doesn't rise
                 like stone shoulders
close and inexhaustible. I am not the city
that raised me. I am the newly ground

sand that shifts with the wind; don't count
on me. I am unstable, unrooted.

*

These three notes, *la la la*, three blue hyacinths floating on a
rock pool.

*

To hell with the small life. I am not exquisite.
Cannot sing like bone china. This is the blue hour.

        I swim in it, alone and perfectly.

Our Man in the Middle East

O Marvel, a garden among the flames!
Ibn 'Arabi

I expected stars, stars that flicker so hard they seem to circle themselves, in love with their own luminosity. Tonight the city, lit like a brain scan transposing our thoughts into brightness and colour, is enough to make shy the bravest constellation. Our man is listening to Brahms' *German Requiem*. It is the soundtrack to Desert Storm, the *son et lumiere* of that war. There's been a rush on milk and chickens, but I know where to find camel's milk still warm from the udder, if that's what it comes to. It won't come to that. How English of me to think warm camel's milk the last straw.

*

We drive north to the mangroves and watch as sand, that may as well have been the world, falls away to green. Then stars. I lie under them, recount the night I taught my son how to find Polaris. It is the story I tell to stitch my life to his. In Hindi, the same stars tell of seven sages. A funeral procession in Arabic. They're Mongolian gods, or hunters chasing the bear, whose blood reddens the autumn leaves. Our man is listening to Lionel Richie as all sides declare victory.

*

It happened one evening, in the great city of Nizwa, that a young guide, more beautiful than the moon, took the woman into the mountains and led her step by rocky step down the canyon to a green lagoon. Her heart was spoken for, and so instead of love, he took pebbles, smooth as rubies from the water, to make a circle around her. In one hand he gave her the stars, the sun he placed in the other. There she sits, safe, outside of time, and utterly alone. With arms full of stars and sun, she can't get up to return to the world, but the world is unimaginable. It must be possible that I, the storyteller, can say what happens next. That in the end she'll throw everything into the air to be at risk again.

*

My heart is a garden, a requiem for the living.
My heart is the fire, and you are the fabled moth

who longs to know what it is to be consumed,
    what it means to be lit from the inside.

*

They've airlifted four thousand dairy cows in, and I am listening to 'Losing My Religion' transposed from minor to major key. I expected to be happier, that brighter scale doing all the work, in love with its own luminosity. Imagine the song is rain. In *Notes on Blindness*, the narrator can hear the shape of the landscape in the fall of the rain, the aural equivalent of light. The geographical equivalent of the present tense. Our man is in love with the light. Bright blue, then brutal. He asks what defeat feels like. *Temporary*, the defeated say.

Overhanging the Only Lake in Catara

From a pink branch of silk floss tree, *come-*
see-me-come-see-me piccolo notes,
woodnotes, brag notes, bidding
the glassy air with his dawning body
notes: the white-eared bulbul to his likeness

Trees

Here is woodsmoke and mirrors,
a thought paused mid-

migration and fed to the parakeet
who sings all the ways this

is not there, and I am neither.
I might be water flooding the wadi

and soaking the samr roots.
Such a delicate tree has no means

to express me, any more than it has
the wherewithal to discard me.

There's a gold souk where the wadi runs,
with a gold raptor in the window.

I've passed it so often, I've named him
Raoul. So you see, I have power.

There are scarlet macaws
in the pet souk, by sacks of rosebuds

and turmeric. Parakeets are ten
a penny, is what I mean.

Trees are like gold, but gold
is like dust. I fall to turning every leaf

and because I don't know
what I'm looking for, I count

the flamingos in their sleep, their pink
heads tucked in their pink bodies –

little pink thought clouds. I think about you
is what I mean, and trees,

how cut in two, a tree is a measure
of weather over time,

each ring an exclamation laid down
in the dark, waiting its day.

from Fairytale No. 2

Meanwhile, the glass butterfly flickers unseen
in the condensed air of a cloud forest
where the tourist plucks petals of a rare
epiphytic orchid for loves me loves me not.
I write anatomically across your body. Do you like
my tongue in your suprasternal notch?
How much your neck reminds me of home.

*

I learn about nakedness from you. *In nakedness*
our needs are clear, our fears natural,
a line you once read and saved for me.
Do I let you name me blackbird?
Your slow enquiry of every feather
and intercostal space becomes my safety.
I have resisted this putting a song in my mouth.

*

Socrates said, if love loves beauty it cannot
itself be beautiful, as we do not desire
what we do not lack. Meanwhile, *I hear you singing*
in the wire … this song plays every day
for a year, two. Are violins the most romantic
instrument or the most anxious?
Not everything asks to be answered, you say.

*

These hot-pink bougainvillea blooms falling
into the backyard. Do they signify
my desire is dying, cyclical, eternal? I am
reckless with it. A man on the radio says depression
is a sickness of desire. It sounds
like a blessing. I read to you knowing my voice
is luminous. Admire me, by all means.

Stanza 2 after John Berger

Love (Eight Movements)

Al-Hawa

I've become concerned with keeping things alive. The flowering cactus on the sideboard is the most still of living things. Its yellow petals will open only the moment before it bursts, over-watered and leaking across the dark veneer. This is not a metaphor. I send you messages and you reply.

Al-Sabwah

Don't tell me there's no birdsong in the desert / tell me the Indian silverbills perch a stem of grass and strip its seed in one movement / hold on /

Al-'Alaqah

The water pools towards the books I haven't yet sent home, only a few now, various histories (of the world, of rain), to better enable my going from this country that is not a refuge but a hovering, a holding, as though placing the bones of the heart in traction.

Al-Kalaf

Elsewhere, in the heart of a compound built on sand, a knotted olive tree, transplanted from Italy and settled next to one bright rose. Don't tell me the rough bark is made lovely by that flower's gaze. Don't tell me how brave you think I am.

Al-'Ishq

The skin gets used to things quickly, to heat and its absence. I'm listening to Max Richter recomposing Vivaldi's *Winter*. Is it snowing where you are? I haven't seen snow for three years. You were there. Briefly, it snowed. Tell me a word more still than "snow".

Al-Najwa

I don't know how to tell you about Richter's *largo*. He makes the violin sound like ice chiming at the almost end of *Dr Zhivago*, which I watched on the plane the last time I left. Do we have to choose between Richter and Vivaldi? They are both only themselves and neither can save us.

Al-Wodd

You and I and two Indian silverbills / their song falling like rain

Al-Huyum

I want to tell you something simple. I want to tell you about the kites. I'll forever associate this exquisite desire to be kind to you with kites. Silk kites the shape of falcons along the Al Corniche, the water lit like loose change and everyone looking up.

About the Human Voice

Telephone

Alexander Graham Bell once said of the telephone, some day, every town will have one. I have three, my UK number, a local one, and a work phone, and I have never needed my phone more or wanted it less. I could've given up my old number. Should have, probably. A chance to weed out all the numbers I never call, that never call me. I guess I'm not ready to disconnect. But it makes me forget sometimes that I am here, and not there, where you are. In *An Affair To Remember*, Cary Grant and Deborah Kerr visit his grandmother who lives in a gorgeous little house cut out of the cliffs overlooking the Mediterranean. Almost entirely isolated, it is where I imagine living one day. I would be completely there and need to be nowhere else. I won't need or want a telephone (except sometimes).

Silence

In *The Guardian* recently, there was an article about a man who broke into a church to pray: "Here the silence creeps into me, a bit like the cold [...] And into that silence I bring all that is not OK with me." Silence and time. August Kleinzahler said technology, as well as being fabulous, has limited our need (and so maybe our capacity) for thinking, memory, association, that it has created "a culture of distraction". Sometimes, when I listen to music, it's because I don't want to be left alone with what is not OK with me, with thinking and memory. If I'm to get any sleep, I want the distraction. Frank Sinatra's *In the Wee Small Hours* is a good bet. His version of 'I Get Along Without You Very Well' is not as painfully beautiful as Nina Simone's. She has a way of singing and playing piano as though those two elements are only barely holding together, like Virginia Woolf's spider's web, and you pay attention, fearing that there's too much felt for such fragility to endure. You can't listen to this for any other reason than for its own sake. If you want to sleep, Frank is lovely. And there's nothing wrong with lovely. Of course, I'm up at 4am comparing these two tracks ... because technology.

Distance

Hey,

I like your observation about distance. Distance in time often appears to create a clarity that wasn't available in the present. The theory goes that our conscious mind, in the moment, is making sense of our actions, rather than determining them. Creating a story of self and the illusion of decision-making. Have you seen the episode of *House* where a guy's had his corpus callosum severed, so his right brain hemisphere and left can't communicate? The guy can't read the instruction "Stand up" because it's on the left side, controlled by the right brain, but his language centre is in the left brain. So instead of reading it, he actually stands up. He doesn't know why, but when asked, he says it's because he's cold and wants to fetch a jumper. His brain has told him a story to make sense of his action.

We rely on memory to make sense of the present. You can't piece together a broken statue head, if it isn't laid down in your memory what a head looks like. To some extent, what we see is what we've seen before.

What we gain from distance, perhaps, temporal and spatial, is the ability to construct a narrative out of the whole mess of crap.

Merry Christmas,
Angelina

Silence

Silence and time and lighting candles. I do this. The *Guardian* writer talks about sitting with God, but I'm there with myself. On the pew I remember sitting on as a child. In the church where I took my first communion. Or as often, along the creek in Castleton, with the little window selling Bradwell's rum & raisin. I'm not sure I like rum & raisin, but it sounds dangerous. I think I'd always choose it. And if I don't believe in a continuous soul, I'm grateful for the illusion. For the story that lets me make sense of myself.

Peak Cavern

Stood facing the cavern's black mouth with the last blue rays snagged on limestone, I look up at the crevice-nests, feathers flickering in the wind. I stand a long time, till the light that offered something like courage is snuffed, the moment gone with the fleeing birds.

Melastoma. Purple flowers
if you eat the fruit
turns your tongue black

melas from the Greek for black
stoma the Greek
for mouth. Melastoma.

That's what it's like to confess. Have you ever made something up just to say to the priest, walked him through some black-lit story of covet and names in vain? *And how long has it been since your last confession?* Right there, in the corner of some backstreet cathedral, tealight bidding prayers blowing in the sanctified cross-breeze. There between the Virgin and a copy of Cafod Weekly. But all that forgiveness. Facing the cavern's black mouth, I flake halfway through the *Our Fathers* to keep from being absolved.

Telephone

On what would have been Chopin's sixtieth birthday, all the major philharmonic orchestras, from the Royal Society to the *Musikverein* in Vienna, programmed an evening of music, so that each would play the 'Minute Waltz' at precisely 7pm GMT. Alexander Graham Bell was in the London audience. In order to play some of Chopin's most intricate pieces, two pianos were required on stage. As the first pianist warmed up, Bell noticed the second piano vibrate. Struck by the beauty of the two pianos vibrating across space, and less literally, across Europe, Bell wondered about the human voice, how wonderful it would be …

Distance

Almost a century later, the composer and pianist Raymond Scott hoped of a time when there would be no need for musicians, only the composer, sitting on stage, able to think his creation directly into the minds of the listeners, untouched, and therefore, unspoilt, by the mediation of players (not "a people person", Kleinzahler says). To have what you wanted to say heard and understood, as you meant it to be heard and understood. That's the dream. Unless it isn't. What if we only had Hoagy Carmichael on stage thinking out his perfect, only, unmediated version of 'I Get Along Without You Very Well (Except Sometimes)'?

In one of my favourite Kleinzahler poems, 'A History of Western Music: Chapter 4', Father Castel develops his 'Clavecin Pour Les Yeux':

and twenty years later, on the 21st of December, 1755, the day of Saint Thomas, patron saint of the Incredulous and Harpsichords […] the Father demonstrated, in a mere half hour of playing, the marvel of his creation: that when C is heard, blue will be seen; when red is seen, E will be heard. And that the *chiaroscuro* will answer to the *grave* D

In the second part of the poem 'Clavecin Pour Le Voyage', Migrenne, "not content with the Father's 'pretty divagations'", aspired "to sit down at his instrument and illuminate the entire map of the world":

Clouds he would color myrrh, sometimes crimson, or for variety an agate or *pigeon neck*. […] Meadows straw color. The sea a pale celadon.

It's a visual representation of sound, a temporal invocation of place. Migrenne uses music as Kleinzahler uses words, placing "a prism over this world, in order to color it with his playing, visiting any one place only so long as the reverberation of a single plucked string." And the listener and the reader are there in this imagined space, mediated by the musician / poet, and by their own longing to be elsewhere.

Confession

Hey,

Yes, I read that St Augustine confessed to stealing pears. His regret was that he'd stolen them without appreciating them, their taste and beauty. That he took them because he could. At least WCW ate the plums. Did you know in China, the word for pear is the same as the word for separation? That for this reason, you should never split a pear with your lover? I confess to spinning a lie. About Chopin and his inspiring A.G. Bell. The truth's rarely as simple as the stories we tell.

I fly home Friday. Feels weird.
Angelina

One Clear Morning After Another

I listen to Nina Simone sing / that fragile final climb of notes /
how she *should never ever think of spring* / and I'm glad to be
where // there's no spring or autumn. / There are trees, but
nothing changes / or nothing changes back / loses its leaves,
greens anew. // How is it done? When Larkin says / *The trees
are coming into leaf* / I see my garden turning green / in my
absence. *Begin afresh*, the trees insist. // But here each night is
like a painting / that you can never know / and I can never not.
Begin afresh. / Or do they mean forget. // Or do they mean,
forgive me so I can forget. / Have I to not forgive the trees / for
what I did not blame them / in order I be remembered?

I have wanted to hear
the silverbill resolve his song
in the winter trees

Correspondences I

١

I'm thinking about your photographs. Nan Goldin thought if she photographed a person or place enough times, she'd never lose them, though it only showed her how much she'd lost. You show me shadows, and I'm grateful, though mostly, this is avoidance. I write you questions like whether the unreliability of memory is preferable to the fixity of a photograph, instead of screaming. The red hibiscus are out. I don't have a photo of this, either.

٢

(Three deer running through an oak valley this side of a river. My house is a few miles the other side. My son lives elsewhere.) I tried to write you about the hibiscus, and the dhow boats drifting into the Gulf, with disco lights and tribute acts singing 'Hotel California', a second language of catchy refrains, but it always became about love. (Did you know in Japan deer can be seen the year through but in poetry connote autumn and melancholy, the stag alone as the sun sets?)

٣

And why shouldn't I write about love? Sometimes the new-moon night is so much like a partial rip in pale blue gauze, I want to eat it.

ɛ

Blue, of course. My young son's favourite colour. I painted the walls of his childhood room Yves Klein Blue. Later he asked for black. I want to talk about the blue slate floor in your photo. Have you read Maggie Nelson on this? The prince of blue's divine and unbuttoned pants? Once my son started bringing his girlfriend home to stay, to be naked in the room next to my son's room distressed me. As though to make space for his desire, my own blew out.

o

I misremember the easy sleep of wanting nothing. I've read they're near to tracing a single memory across the brain. I would watch my neural pathway light up as I recollect being held. Or you could paint the way 'Mr Blue Sky' flickers between lobes separated from its meanings to me. Carl Sagan said we're like butterflies who flutter for a day and think it's forever. I'm thinking of coming home. This morning I woke reciting the words my grandson's mother says to him, holding him close as he cries for no clear reason. *You're fine. You're fine. You're fine.*

Fairytale No. 19

It has taken me oak trees   oak trees belligerent
from seed to sapling

                        to realise –
it's taken me oak trees   away   from home
from honey   away

                    to realise   how dance   how disco
how damaged I am   I am

                            afraid of everything
everything.   I have been   in filigree or figurine
since   in furs, in figment

                                in fleeting
or floodlight since

                    I recounted the apple I was suturing
and my mouse didn't bless me

                        and my faun lifted

                    to protect his own skitter
which meant I had to go to the cove

    and because I was willing   to go to the cove
                    to protect
as no one else was protecting   me   I was treated
like a balance perversion   a balalaika

                            like a bagatelle
my dormouse   tender to believe me
if I dropped the charlestons.

                            Long before,
I learnt to plant for darlings
to anticipate   all the schemas of each deadbeat
to try to mitigate them   in how I behaved.

    I do this   all the tinctures.
All the timpanists.   Obsessively.   It's exhausting.

Correspondences II

What do you see from your window? Here, an apartment block rises within the footprint of an older home, the interior of a half-bulldozed wall, half-mosaics, murals in amber and snapdragon, an archaeology of sorts. Gardens grow out of sand, are tended minute to minute. They seem unchanging. They seem dug over every night and planted new by morning, pricking pretty holes in the always gold light.

I am not anxious
only full of butterflies

prettifying the structures
of my heart and stomach

I am so lucky
to be so pretty inside

Let me tell you about the trees transplanted from Argentina and made to survive. I admire the aspiration of a manmade hill. The way a pearl diver measures time by the lungful, I sit under the neem tree in fifty degrees, till just before I pass out. What I really want to show you is the scarring – (see) how the sea spray begins to rust the flowers.

The Flight Home

The pale folds and erosion of Iranian mountains. It's a solitary thing to look down and see snow so close to the desert. Like a seaside town out of season, to return everything to the familiar, a night of two-foot snow along the coast, the soft ground giving to your weight. Salt air will reveal sand by morning, but in these minutes before sleep, the world is miraculous, and you are safe in its smallness. *Let's stay here, call this home.* But you didn't stay. In an hour the curvature of Earth will arc blue-orange as you fly through the second where day and night meet. If the plane could hold its speed you'd live inside this instant, like a thought between words or what occurs in the space from sight to perception. There will be rain. A perturbation of green-grey rivers and faces. You lent a blue-eyed echo of your own face to the hills, left teeth-marks like runes in the limestone. So tell me this – if you saw yourself in the rock formations, what are you afraid of, the profundity of arrival, or its lack, in the lights dimmed for descent?

Snow Has Come

Home-sickness for my little dwelling has come upon my mind
(Irish, 12th century: author unknown)

A quietness falling on my small house. And the fuchsia that
keeps on well into winter. I wasn't there to cut it back, or to
watch the settling of things. Snow delineates before it covers,
so that nothing is absent, nothing ever settles, *the calves in the
plain, the deer on the moor.*

Hellebore

Correspondences: Silence

When Cristofori invented the piano, he created the mechanism
that makes the hammer fall away and not rebound to sound
the string again. I tell you this thinking about the man who set fire
to his piano and played its collapsing frame the length
of Debussy's *Clair de lune* – but also because of a child's hand
that slips from his mother's and into his own son's fingers,
the force of that (grand)mother's impulse to sound the string again.
All her names mean mother, the way Sontag comes to read
what a photograph should say in light of what's passed. She
is talking about catastrophe, and this is not in any real sense
a catastrophe. What is not temporary, love? My love is like a piano
in flames, playing in plumes of D flat major. My love
is the catabolic drift of moonlight and smoke, the accompanying
part-song of blackbirds. It is the opposite of silence
(an original, inanimate state), the effort it takes to hold quiet.

Fairytale: The Purple Iris

I don't believe in ghosts but there are other hauntings. The long-stemmed irises in my mother's day vase, a hieroglyphic haunting in one's own home, alone and ok with that. Each fresh iteration transposes what's been, adds rooms and paint, a sampling of wallpaper like a musical phrase, or a bird that flies inside by mistake before heading out with this new knowledge.

Do you desire how I in bloom
become one thing? What will die with me?
Without consolation, thought-spores
like pollen, fill the room

The noise a person makes, dying, preverbal and full of fluid. Her own rhythm, intonation. Kepler believed the planets each had their own pitch, defined by their orbits' nearest and furthest points from the sun. Mercury sings soprano, the earth alto, and so on. The maternal earth singing to its children. A shadow passing the end of the bed hours before she's gone – I think about this. Is this the weight of the soul lifting? It is possible not to believe in the soul and to speak of a woman being both inside her body, with its tethers and heat, and outside time in this absence of syntax, which is not an absence of meaning but of convention, the city street-lit like a string of questions climbing the hills. A daughter catching her mother in this here-and-there state might ask what she hopes to understand, or in the cadence and metre of this last language, return to the echolalia of her first. Leaves repeating the last summer's leaves. To buy flowers, then, is to understand the nature of motherhood. There is nothing unnatural about the iris's slow-at-first falling into its constituent parts.

Fairytale: The Hathersage Road

Tiny white moths in the bracken and heather flit up like delicate, anxious thoughts. You ask if I'm as well as I seem, and I tell you about the wild-tiger butterfly, low along the bedding plants and irrigated dust. I want to make this picture for you to speculate to and from – to have been so much in the desert, and still surrounded by colour. I map my hyper-vigilant body apportioned between the sand and hibiscus, as though in dialogue. As though the sand were the unconscious of trees.

A mountain apollo, not to be held in cupped hands
but separate from yourself, like a psalter split in two

and sold into different collections. To read one half
is to call to the other, to have it answer

So much has been given to the consideration of blue. These harebells, for example. Berger says blue is both adorning and modest, *the robe of the Madonna*. That through the sway of these conflicting ideals, in blue we find the erotic. Does this allude to the eternal paradox of mother as virgin? Were the two women given the same name in that story to grant our fantasy of the maternal body, as well as its human urgency? I divide the colours of my desire against the sedge and gritstone, not for you to acquire or reject, but in awe of this fragmented light, without hope of resolution.

Fairytale: The Escapologist

i.

What would I be without this loan   this load
this living with accuracy   would I be more or less

though I've never considered this dance a gift
this dandelion   a gift

          When I watch the finch
I become aware of how devastating it is to me
to see an epoch   not in tinderboxes
   not in timpanists of darling
       you might imagine in the desert
               but in everyday

I can't see the finch without knowing the ruse
the run-up   When I go for a walk
      it's my realist to choose
the shortest   not because I'm tired
or have somewhere else to be   but because
to ward off is to take away my capacity for return

     I thrill   I thrash   I threat about this
about what this might mean   to always
            have an echo on the exit

ii.

The lotus nymph turns herself into a tree, her pink, hysterical flowers describing her trauma to those who hear the language. The rest of us see beauty where the story has fallen away. There are contemporary manifestations, with modern names, such as psychogenic non-epileptic seizures, that can wrap a person's thoughts in ivy. In the meandering spine of a tree hit by lightning to grow across the slow, impassive river, she is both above and below the surface, offering her return gaze in a knot of green elder.

iii.

The fable of the two trees: a plum tree singing the opening lines of Patti Smith's 'Gloria', in counterpoint to the Peggy Lee of a wild purple buddleia. *Play the guitar. Play it again, my Johnny.* Vienna, in her white dress, sits equidistant between them, figuring the equation that reconciles innocence with survival. It is a reworking of the scene where she plays the piano against that ochre backdrop and the black suits of the law, absolved by Johnny of the last five years, but made to stand for the crimes of others. Is she demonstrating her innocence or her isolation? At least in isolation, her sins, if that's what they are, are her own. What drives a person to the clean waters of the film's end? *Jesus died for somebody's sins but not mine*, the plum tree sings. To be cleansed. Resurrected. My sins intact.

iv.

And like this, this reservoir walled with stone and thistle
reflecting ourselves back to ourselves, or how shame
sits at the centre of things, like the first cuckoo in spring.

Postcard

… and the violence
of this periwinkle shell

its syntax too soon
spun to a point

as though change
were always so sudden

completely itself
(as sea oak is)

to climb inside
its inner expanse

an inarticulate floating
to add weight

in lieu of love
which is only a word

Postcard

… or the snow-anonymous
woods spotted

with stinking hellebores
a path of evergreen

breadcrumbs recover
the way, the way home or

not home, hellebore
shaking its purple fringe

as I hum *A Love
Supreme*, four notes

of the double bass
repeated, the way a person

learns to speak again
to mouth the O

of over, open, disobedient
hellebore, unbidden

alters its gaze
in light of my gaze

Fairytale: The Vanishing Point

You like stories, and so I want to tell one. These things never begin at the beginning. We'll start with the space it occupies. It is off-centre, like Titian's Madonna, which is not so much a distancing but a progression, the vanishing point behind her as she moves to the head of the stairs. However we try to separate ourselves from the mother, we are all always looking up. It is a space to hold us, as though safe. Or, it is a space that makes versions of us possible. When we tell our mothers what we want, we're asking to be forgiven, or to become a rendering of ourselves we believe worth forgiveness. This is not the story I want to tell, but it contains all the others, elemental as love. We swim in it.

Not the cupboard, the old mother says,
but the space around it. A blackbird's song circumscribes
the silence at the centre of things.

I climb the stairs in my own home, as if this were an ending, my son's old room ahead of me. What if the spider in Paula Rego's drawing, huge and looming, is not the mother but the girl in reflection? Why else has she not run off from her tuffet, but sits there face to awful face? She, too, looks up. Would this imply that the mother is an aspect of herself, and that this aspect is monstrous? Without intention, my love, he goes, and I tell him, *go on*, and mean it. And in the mirror, a dog rose climbing its chaotic way to the light, hot-pink, her easy expression, the rage she must feel to cut so thoroughly.

Correspondences: The Lark Ascending

I would tell you about the composer, who worked on his *Lark* before and after a war, that between those years, between the original and its revision, he drove a military ambulance. That each alteration pasted over the previous notes, erased that old reality, as though it never happened. Which of course, it didn't. Or Schafer's composition of snow, his sketches of snowdrifts crossing a stave like memory traces sung and settling through the winter trees. There's comfort in the weight of snow, the voices that layer and hum, a sudden dark as they open their mouths – *ah*. All this time I've been waiting for dawn when I already had what I needed. Do you want to hear how trauma transforms the freedom of a lark? This lark that's so in love with the land. Perhaps the violin is the bird. The piano is the earth. The intervals between them like an expanse of air that grows, diminishes, equivocates. Or is the lark a projection of the earth's subliminal self, a haunting without significance beyond this reaching upwards?

Correspondences: Song

There's pleasure in looking at this lamp, its stem turned from an old mill's bobbin. The shade I chose. There's pleasure in choosing. Its repurposing literally shines. Come look at this small joy with me, the warm-white bulb I twisted into its socket like a spring flower.

*

When Etel Adnan wrote *Sea and Fog*, she was living in California: "Look well at the Pacific before you die. The best of the promised paradises have neither its hues nor its splendor". That she looked on what was in front of her, its handful of notes.

*

What is it I want to say about the deer scratching at my door that can't be said to your face, and the pond only mistaken for stagnant, its surface of still leaves, a life-ring nailed too high to a tree, blooming orange rose, lovely and without intent?

*

Two portraits. Helen standing on white roses, Cassandra on red. De Morgan paints the fall of the cloth from the line of the body as though it is my body, the linen against my skin. What this means remains simple – but to say it. To say it, simply.

*

Afternoons, the sun hits the stained glass, avows, for a while, a red rose on my wall. To become the tree that tenders both white and red roses, or the absence implied in naming those branches, a silence inscribed with fragrance, aphids.

*

To have brought a shell to bed with me, picked from a Welsh cove. To have spoken to no one, to have let grammar abrade and brighten with the wet stones. To return now with something to tell you. "The sea", says Adnan. "Nothing else".

Postcard

… but not so dear as a tree
or a lover to salvage

what's left but the sea
let close, closer and over

and over, to hold the black-
black stone's shiny

face to your face and find
yourself not reflected

back but pressed and held
inside the jet's core

with its own old self
like memory or sculpture

Postcard

... if not the sea, rain
blowing the stone's faces

back into the rock
smooth and unintelligible

or not unintelligible
but wilfully misheard

or if not wilfully, wanting
nothing from you

its great arched
shoulders and stained-

glass memory
cow parsley growing

between its gaping bones
to sit with it, grieve

what's gone, or love this
new, reckless body

Fairytale: The Blackbird

That disconnect
between the moving mouth of the blackbird
and its song as it reaches my ear.

I tell a daughter her mother has died.
Her grief fills the room with flowering quince
which grows in the poorest soil.

What do you believe in, if not in ghosts
the rapid breathing of a blackbird
building its nest in your lungs

a foreignness made from feathers
and passed down like dark hair.

Home now, I undress alone and stand
under the shower, the soap-smell of blossom,

strange to myself, this song in my mouth
as good a song as any

Postcard

… and then the news
falling, still, in counterpoint

of rhododendron leaves
or sifting of mauve

as if all we wanted
were meaning, and not this

universal giving way
this flinging off

or the longing to have
no further to go

that in these absurd days
to drop to the earth

not for love of our
own roots, the conjecture

of grass, the flies that rise
and lower in assent

Correspondences III

But what if nature is not consolation but the matrix or code that holds our collective memory? Or not the matrix in opposition to reality, but in reality, consoling. Am I a woman dreaming I'm an emerald moth or a moth dreaming I'm a woman?

[…]

When Hendrix told Patti Smith about his version of Woodstock, he imagined a universal language of musicians playing and playing, adjusting imperceptibly to each other, like gathering waves, or not the waves but wildflowers thrown out to sea, returning now in dialogue. Does this sound like heaven to you? If you translate the word "esperanto" into English, it is embedded with hope. Tell me everything […]

[…]

It's true. I align myself with what is beautiful and wretched, separate from and in sight of my body, because the sea is how I think about loss. There are other ways. In what way can an ancient wood tell of a child that's lost in a story that doesn't resolve but is deciduous as language? Entirely unfound, she seems the opposite of this border I press my hands to. I am both desired and undesirable, while she is merely, utterly elsewhere. We are each, though, caught between autonomy and return. There's another wood, where children are named in song and she can hear the clarinet cuckoo of her mother's call above the trees, as far as the shore. This is her loss. To have never been at risk. Three prisms placed over love, and the swell so calm as a consequence of kelp beds close to the harbour, and nothing to do with us.

[...] Compare the pink thrift clustering towards the cliff's edge with Mapplethorpe's arrangement of tilted tulips. To be composed by you was heaven. To know myself only through representation, contained, repeatable. He was right, do you think, that beauty and the devil are the same thing?

from Fairytale No. 24

I beg your pardon ... politely the radio takes back
its promises, offers rain in lieu, though if a rose garden could be
offered at all, the rain, and the notes falling like rain
like seeds, or seed-small for the birds to eat or let fall over
another's yard, to bed-in between flagstones
and the song ends, and the table between us, as though love
were a table we sit at, the flowers in the vase.

Correspondences: The Rhododendron Tree

There's a second in the film of *The Snows of Kilimanjaro* when the backdrop comes loose, tipping the riverbank into the corner of the screen, and if we held our disbelief in abeyance until now, it would be hard to ignore this, this tilted horizon that reveals not the real world but the dream. How did we evolve to beguile ourselves so wholly, to imagine ourselves central and rhapsodic in saturated colour? Is it because we desire the landscape we marginalise, as though being the one desired should bring you to your knees, or that I, in my desire am ashamed, and so shame? When I think about this, I'm not thinking about you. But the word *dream*, with its capacity to signify one thing and its opposite, brings me back to my own small rhapsodic heart, which is nothing like a solution but a restating of the problem.

*

Or, do I believe in dreams not as desire, that they are not so much the longed for depicted in a Roman mosaic and buried under the modern vine, but the Roman goddess of love and abundant wine reaching her finger out to mine, like the touch of Creation, or an osprey lurching towards its prey? To reconstitute the fragments of an old question, then, is love a divine gift or a memory we dream to recover?

*

Both the book and the film open with this riddle, that the body of a leopard lies at the summit and no one knows why it was there. I imagine the leopard's coat still shining above the snow, its gold lovely in contrast, though without its bodily heat, the snow must bury the corpse. It's the repression of a leopard I have in mind, how the film makes us complicit in a lie when Gregory Peck's character survives the ending, betraying the physical laws of his own narrative. Do we mistake dream for fantasy, shame for love? What is it we're trying to save? To ask another way, imagine the wind chime sounding in my garden, the sparrow-pitch of its blue glass leaves – *chirrup chirrup* – for last year's fruit still shrivelled on the branches. Do you recognise this underlying language of desire, or only the late light turning on the glass? The relationship between the dream and the waking is one of Freud's first questions.

*

Freud tells us Aristotle thought a man's dreams reflected his bodily, more than psychic, health. To walk in his sleep under the burning sun might pre-empt a pyrexia, and so I've begun asking my patients about their dreams each morning. They take it as being a kindness, a general interest in how they slept, and I let them. Why not? But in the logs I'm making, I'm hoping to find a significance between the stories they tell and their cardiovascular observations, as a form of early warning score. Perhaps they spend the night running from a falcon only to develop an atrial flutter. Or they hear the opening strum of Van Morrison's 'Sweet Thing' just before they wake. And later, a rush to the head, or feeling of relief. In Oliver Sacks's case studies, he meets a New York grandmother who, after a stroke, had temporal lobe seizures that filled her ears with Irish songs. She, though, suffered from reminiscence, and as such, can't help us with preventative medicine.

*

At my grandmother's funeral, my uncle says
too English for India, too Indian for England.

*

In one of Rousseau's *Solitary Walks* he buys all the apples from a girl at the fair and gives them away to a half-dozen boys. Rebecca Solnit describes how he was practicing his defence for an imaginary trial, charged with abandoning his own children. But for all the happy moments he recalls in his walk, it is shot through with persecutory thoughts. No amount of evidence absolves him. Whatever we think we're guilty of, and we are (sometimes) guilty, it's only a placeholder for some deeper shame. What if guilt is (sometimes) only a rhododendron tree flowering mindlessly along the riverbank? What if these flowers were there from the start, a haunting, perhaps, their pink heads bending towards their own reflection, exiled under their own weight?

*

Dysmetria is the inability to judge distance. It is a function of the cerebellum, to know when to stop.

*

I dream in fragments of *Rhapsody in Blue*
the opening phrase never descending
to answer its own question. I dream in notations

of wildflowers, the iolanthe's quiet dissent
against the clamouring larkspur, the Shepard Tone
of time in dreams, rising, always rising

*

Do you remember that early episode of *The West Wing*? Cartographers for Social Equality show CJ the Gall-Peters Projection, where the relative size of the continents is rendered accurately. Africa is huge (and potentially, upside down), and yet, it was on the radio yesterday, as though this is news. The world is as imaginary as it ever was. How strange we're struggling to flatten the earth after waiting so long to learn it's round. But if the Peters Projection is criticised for its distortions of shape and distance, there's a beautiful butterfly map that shows the world unfolding from an octahedron. Africa and South America, like facing forewings, spread out over the rest. You and I are barely there, and as though asking the stars to define my place, I'm happy to be found so harmless.

*

Harmless, no. That we recite stories equating size with power may or may not be the fault of the old maps, but it is perpetuated by them. In another Solnit book, she says: *We think we tell stories, but stories often tell us, tell us to love or to hate, to see or be blind* … She has a story about a roomful of apricots stripped from her mother's tree. They are, she says, her birthright, her fairy tale quest. Across the pages some of the fruit begin to rot. Others are preserved and sent to friends. That story doesn't belong to me, but it does flicker through the one I want to tell you, about the trauma we're gifted, pass on.

*

There's a vintage shop that's always closed, and a jug in the window. I imagine it holding a handful of purple irises. It's shaped like a savoy cabbage, its handle wrought from ropes of corn, but it's not the shape that makes me hungry. It might be the colour or glaze, but whatever else this hunger is, it is also only hunger. I've felt it before, as a child reading *Rapunzel*. The witch's garden made me want, as the young mother did, what didn't belong to me. No shame, child. I became aware of my small round stomach, how it could be sucked into nothing, and I could disappear. The inverse was also true. Mostly I want to hold the jug. There's harmony in its overlapping leaves. I am ravenous with it. I felt it again tonight when I read 'Strawberry Fields' was made by combining two songs in different keys, one sped up, the other slowed until almost, almost perfect. And there it is, I want to tell you, the harmony of the continuous soul blown wide open.

*

When his daughter calls out from a dream, *Anna Freud,*
strawberries, wild strawberries, he says, she's using her name
to take possession of what she's been denied that day.
But he also says that dreaming of fruit
of apples, cherries, or a half-eaten pear, signifies desire
for the mother's breast, to feed from it, to be it.
To both possess and be possessed by what has been forbidden.
Do we ever learn to live with less? The literal work
of keeping the apricots from going to waste. I want this.

*

Angela Pelster tells us that Indian Yellow was, perhaps,
introduced there from Persia, and made from the urine of cows
that ate nothing but mangoes. She describes how Vermeer's
paintings glow with it, as though they're lit from within.
(This phrase applies to other fruits. Plath's blackberries. Or is
it the meadows? Kleinzahler's peaches.) What I like about the
Vermeer passage is what she says he understands: *the way a red*
dress was never only red, but smoldering blue inside its shadowed
folds; the way a wall was pockmarked with light, with every color
in the room layered beneath it. Her mother's favourite colour is
yellow. She says this is because she's Dutch. Because of
Vermeer. I read this essay years ago, but in rereading it occurs
to me, as though for the first time, that my family are as Dutch
as they are Indian, and so I move through my house looking
for evidence, for yellow. A cushion or vase. It's hard, she says,
when looking at a beautiful thing, to know where the beauty
is coming from.

*

Sacks describes the movement of a patient's paintings
from figurative to abstract as the pathology of the occipital lobe.
This man no longer thinks in images, dreams in them.
And if he might acknowledge the colour yellow
or the geometry of a globe, strawberries, or his wife's face,
the soul it expresses, are lost to him. To be unable
to perceive the whole, or your own whole in relation to it.
Is this the same as wanting nothing? I dreamt the blue nude
of Georgia O'Keeffe's stepped out from the print
on my bedroom wall, climbed under the covers, held me.
I dream in blue and green. In rhythm. I dream in jazz drums,
a kind of rain or echolocation, the reverberation
of desire sketched across the blue-night shoreline, presenting
itself in blue waves, always coming, closer, closer.

Postcard

… so to make a soft bed
of gingko and alder

as though to hold Medusa's
head while I wash

my hands, this monster
we carry and can't

pronounce, loud
and distant, a note above

the stave for the horn
to erase the sound it creates

or the candlesnuff fungus
that lights, revises

the buddleia stump
with its own insistent love

Fairytale: Rain

A woman's tongue was shot with an arrow when she spoke of her own beauty, and though the tongue is vascular, I think, rather than blood loss, it was the loss of language that killed her. That to be unable to say what we want, to be unable to name desire even to yourself, is something a person might die from. The world we experience is drawn from what's caught in the lines of language. If we had the word for walking against the wind for fun, wouldn't we be less inclined to envy, more able to love? That in such a world made possible by language and weather, we'd be happy? A tongue might be rebuilt. Even a damaged language centre can find new pathways to speech. Think of a tree cut back to the ground, how with time and rain, this coppiced wood might be absolved, learn regrowth. The foliage, though it continues to lean into the light, isn't the same as it was. The network of sap that nurtures it isn't the same, and perhaps the altered acidity of the soil has turned your pink blossom blue, your conceivable world changed with these new linguistic birds and insects.

Correspondences: Oak

after James Canton

With each ending, he returns to the ancient oak
until he is, perhaps at last, alone. He talks about sailing
too far from the tree, and I think this anchoring
                saves him. He's telling me what I need
though I'm aware of how much I'm looking
exactly for this.
                      The comfort is in the illusion
of constancy. Or, is it in the seasonal, the falling, again?
You touch my arm as you walk by. By this
I mean only to register an encounter
                which is how we mean at all.

*

Think of the canopy as delimiting this space
where such an encounter is possible. Under its cover
the conditions provide the ghost life
of bats and birds
              that would, he says, have been here
had all the oaks survived.
When you slip your hand into my pocket
                    when I let you
we open a dialogue both with each other and
with these ghost birds, the bullfinch
           lamenting the morning sun.

*

Not constancy, then, but longevity.
That's what he's saying about *oak knowledge*.
To rest a hand on the tree and feel its outlasting calm

the slow rhythm of eight-hundred years.
To mark time with the turning inwards in snow
                                the dismantling of leaves.
Are we changed in this, exposed as we are?
                What is this need to hold my body
against something more lovely
                                        against more than myself?

*

I've become aware of the disconnect between my body
and the stories it tells. I am dominated by
                                and change the oak
the way a nesting owl lines its tree hole
        alters the surrounding air with its call.
But an owl that thinks itself tree. Tells tree stories.
                        Grows to the shape of the wind.

*

What do we want from each other, if not each other, *each oak's
own oakness*?

*

The oak reading is mapped against the recomposing
of Vivaldi's *Spring*. It is possible to talk about this
                in the same terms as the tree
how the composer had to see the music, feel the strings
                  as though they were his own
to meet them, suddenly
be moved by them, before he could transform them.
                          Not equals, but there was love.
The ways we leave each other changed
            a violin phrase caught in the branches.

Correspondences: Against the Blue of Longing, the Proximity of Green

Japonica grips tight to its little leaves, a bottle of Chartreuse held to the light. Japonica leaves like small print, details. Parakeet-green pieces of torn paper shaking in the wind. To recognise Japonica is to know it again, as though something laid down in memory surfaces with its flowering, a cluster of pink pressed between pages, and now, years later, recovered. This is all I wanted to say, the simplest thing about love, that it is possible to know a stranger again, the calming vanilla of old books, a name unearthed, the stem preserved.

Credence

for RML

from Fairytale: Study for the hopeful on underglaze
painted ceramic

    … to be carried through the woods
to a stagnant millpond and filled

with frogspawn and algae, my blue
and white porcelain holding water
and waiting to see something alive.

It is possible the way cobalt blue
travelled to make something beautiful
out of something broken is the same

as how a person might break a vase,
the long-stemmed iris falling
to the floor as the breaker tries to cup

the tumbling water that is already
                  winding back to the river …

Love (Six Rituals)

To Blow

You can't make taro edible without a little work. Look how lovely this pestle with the bird's head handle, its wings in the wind. How much like today with its worn-smooth stone. You touch me without purpose as I walk by. The bird in its extraneousness.

The Thorn

A model of four cows descended from the Egyptian gods and still their fingerprints pressed into the clay. The Egyptians identified the auditory nerve as how the soul enters the body. Does the soul sound like tall grass, like water rushing and the chattering stones, like the stories we tell? You lay yourself out in language for me, words like bones waiting to take on the shape of wild cattle.

Red

A garland of chillies. A garland of bright charred chillies around the god of a divine food. Her lips parted mid-breath. A god of maize that loves enough to lose her head with the harvest, trusting a return with the new crop. Don't worry about me. I am immortal with trust.

To Spread a Camel with Tar

Obsessional to love whoever held this clay pot, hand-wove these patterns into its side to mimic the knots of a cherry tree, the interlacing of fishbones. To hear the stories spoken above the water boiling in its belly each evening. To love the one who, in rediscovering its initial beauty, thousands of years later, thought to add this lining of gold leaf.

And Reaches the Spleen

Or these lovers carved into a pebble. Their eyeless faces. Look how lovely their gaze as close as barley stalks wrapped round each other by the breeze. Or not just stalks but trees. Or not trees but attendants, dancing greenly, lichen-covered and pressing near to hide this shared and lovely affliction, from the god that would eat its own children, and would love their bones.

To Perish, Happily

A colony of bats flies inside to eat the flora and flourishing bugs from the heart, as though the chaos of wings could undo this gnarl with their opening, opening.

On Listening to *My Baby's Taking Me Home* by Sparks

A house in which rain does not fall, a place in which spears are not feared, as open as if in a garden without a fence around it.
(Irish, 9th century: author unknown)

Home, like a ritual. Like a hat taken off, head lowered at the back step, my breath held to hear the song more clearly. A sort of peace in the repeated word falling as leaves on the mat. I am exposed to its element, even as I try to shape this word to stone so carefully in my mouth. To dovetail my feet into the floorboards, the lights gone on like the ink flourish of a signature. And then someone, blown in, the altered note that unsettles walls, uproots joists, that makes what was ordinary exquisite.

A sudden blackbird on the broken trellis
its broken song flowering here
and here, one repeated lyric unconsciously

beautiful like the clematis that returns
each year with no idea of how glad I am

In asking you to love it, I am, of course, asking you to love me, though that word loses meaning the more it's used, while the song only grows more eloquent. Is this loss what happened to *god*? Like the Vikings minting Christian coins and spelling St Petri with Thor's axe, as though the rise of one religion and the demotion of another to mythology met in quivering peace. Here too, there's repetition, the notion of god continuous even as it changes, while the word *god* stays the same. But if there's a parallel of attenuation between the language of god and love, isn't there also our desire to be held, to be home, to lower our gaze and read intentionality into the soil?

Postcard

… but the always
already greygreen sea

as though kindness
were always this wild

the salt-spindrift
like snow blown

in lieu of an opening move
and now these two

whale's teeth
like chess pieces waiting

to march back
into the ocean

to be loved
by their element

a return, a necessity
a question of space

between them
or not space –

a holding –
to be pulled under

guzzled and sudden
to be changed

the way you turn
towards me, or we turn

towards each other
carved into queen

and king by the coral
and current

Correspondences: The Credence of Birds

A gritstone edge. Boulders higgledy-piggledy with sprouts of purple heather. No sun to speak of but light diffuse and silver, an evenness to it. Maybe rain, if there's the wherewithal. Or a sort of shimmer to the flattened grass, as though rain has been. An absence left. A man in a red anorak, a bouldering mat folded on his back, walks quickly right to left. If Heaney's chorus of boulder-still birds beginning to stretch from under their shawls can be made as lovely as he wrote it, do it. Pheasants, falcons. A spray of meadow pipits darting out from their hair and hands. Chip-chip-chip-chip. A woman climbs the rocks toward a platform stage-right, with the silhouette of an ancient fort just about suggested. The birdsong continues – ek-ek-ek-ek – but she is alone. Perhaps she addresses herself. Or perhaps, someone else. Someone absent. No questions, but the fractals in the bracken, their green mathematics transposed as music, the closing cadence that resolves the song.

She:

I might believe that a kingfisher strung up on silk can predict the weather, or that placing the semen of a pigeon on someone's shirt can make that person love you. You think it's wild, but you believe time runs as the crow flies. Take the roses replanted to my new house, those roses that know a home before this, my young son, the woman I was, its stems grown long and winding through the pale fuchsia, the fuchsia with its pale pink memory of a previous owner. The latitude of these two recollections mapped in space, in gradients, and tangled into a grammar of now, or here, the woman I am. I would send you their late bloom like a temple tumbling into the sea to keep in your wallet with the present tense and the half built, a botanical representation of time, the ongoing of what's gone inscribed in the ground underfoot.

Chorus:

sip-sip-sip-sip

A cage in the side of a boulder opens. A Japanese tit flies out and across the water. A stone arch at the back of the stage, where the river runs down to the orchestra pit. Hanging from the stone, an iron hook and a small bell. The bird rings the bell and collects a folded piece of paper that could be your fortune from the hook, flies into the gods. Let it go.

She:

I would send you John Cale's 'Big White Cloud'. *After all is said and done / everything is just like it began.* But time flows one way, whatever leaves it gathers in its talons, and to predict is to look back, to believe that autumn will cause the trees to redden. Bergson says that what we express is the dead leaves floating on the surface of the water, the various and fugitive reduced to the same handful of words, as though love isn't changed by having loved. I don't know what this means for us. Perhaps, that's the point. The reds and golds were always there, it's only that we see them now. *Everything's clear, everything's bright.* To leave this unspoken way of being unspoken, and so unchanged by language that can only approximate how it feels, to dream in birdsong, the water trickling down from the moors.

The chorus boulders huddle against the cold – chee-chee-chee-chee
– Light fades to black – ek-ek-ek-ek

Reindeer

If the question about the sound of a falling tree is really about the offering of sound and the validity of that offering against the impossibility of being heard, and the tree is really my body falling for yours, even as your body is absent, in its offering is it possible my body is loved? I would make an origami tree for you, not to show you the world but to create one you might choose for yourself, thick twisting branches that could hold us above the river with all its light and silvering sticklebacks, like coins thrown into the water for luck. Would this holding help? Or perhaps the falling is the nature of sound and we can only risk the river. I would carve you the full autumn antler of two reindeer swimming the length of a mammoth's tusk, the one hoping the other still follows unable to turn her head. He knows the wet smell of her carved fur, that he couldn't change his course without shattering them both. What does she see except the empty space ahead? Into that air she conjures his face, precise as the equation of water forming on cold glass, and the knowledge, that in their precariousness, the bone will shatter. The nature of falling, is then, a sort of self-destruction, a sort of giving in as the gazelle to the lion, the reindeer to the river, or not giving in but the rushing towards, the way water rushes to spew and lose itself at the mouth, this urgency to be drunk down, to be sea-numbed cold, that holds within it the inevitability of starting again.

Postcard

I am writing to you / all the time, I am writing // with both hands /
day and night
Franz Wright

                        … but my mind
on this river about to overrun
     run and pocket the leaves in its rush
                    narrowing what constructs
we'd hoped would mean
                something akin to what's felt.
There's peace
                    in letting it come
        in lowering my head to the current
                its lustrous not thinking
how gravity still holds.
The two of us small
                            against its orbit.
I'm thinking about you
                    all the time, the way
water doesn't think about running.
I'm thinking about you
                        with both hands …

Notes

The **epigraph** ('No more the slippery cloudlike moon') is taken from 'Jars of Springwater' by Rumi, in *Rumi: The Big Red Book*, trans. Coleman Barks (HarperCollins, 2010).

Correspondences

In **Fairytale No. 17**, the soprano is Irina Lungu and she is talking about *La traviata* on *Tales from the Stave*, broadcast on BBC Radio 4 on 6 May 2017.

The song in **Lullaby** is the Wexford Lullaby (12th century with new words added by John Renbourn). The version I was listening to is sung by Jackie Oates.

Frangipani. Of course the Argo myth doesn't belong to Maggie Nelson's *The Argonauts* (Graywolf Press, 2015), but her book influenced the writing of the poem, so I wanted to include something of that influence. She's quoting Barthes at the end, here: "Just as the Argo's parts may be replaced over time but the boat is still called the Argo, whenever the lover utters the phrase 'I love you,' its meaning must be renewed by each use, as 'the very task of love and of language is to give to one and the same phrase inflections which will be forever new'".

The epigraph to **Our Man in the Middle East** is from Poem 11 of Ibn 'Arabi's *Tarjumān al-ashwāq*, translated by Michael A. Sells. Our Man is Jeremy Bowen, and his personal history was broadcast on BBC Radio 4 in 2017. *Notes on Blindness* (2016), directed by Peter Middleton and James Spinney, profiles the writer and theologian John M. Hull.

Overhanging the Only Lake in Catara. The sound of the bulbul is described in *Common Birds of Qatar* (Frances Gillespie, 2011) by Hanne & Jens Eriksen and Frances Gillespie.

Fairytale No. 2. '*In nakedness...*' is an intentional misquotation from Theatre de Complicite, *Mnemonic* (1999). '*I hear you singing in the wire*' is from 'Wichita Lineman' (written by Jimmy Webb, performed by Glen Campbell).

In **About the Human Voice**, the 'article about a man who broke into a church' is by Giles Fraser (*The Guardian*, 5 January 2017). The August Kleinzahler extracts are taken from his collections *Music: I-LXXIV* (Pressed Wafer Press, 2009) and *The Strange Hours Travelers Keep* (Faber and Faber, 2004).

Nina Simone's line in **One Clear Morning After Another** is taken from her version of 'I Get Along Without You Very Well' (written by Hoagy Carmichael). The poem also incorporates two short quotations from 'The Trees' by Philip Larkin (in *High Windows*, Faber and Faber, 1974).

Correspondences I is informed by Nan Goldin's *Couples and Loneliness* (Korinsha Press, 1998), Maggie Nelson's *Bluets* (Wave Books, 2009), and Carl Sagan's *Cosmos* (Random House, 1980).

Correspondences I and **II** are written in response to work by artist Mark Rowan-Hull: https://rowan-hull.com/practice/correspondences/

The epigraph to **Snow Has Come** appears in *A Celtic Miscellany* (Penguin, 1971), selected and translated by Kenneth Hurlstone Jackson. The italicised line at the end (*the calves in the plain, the deer on the moor*) is taken from the same poem in the anthology.

Hellebore

Correspondences: Silence was written after watching 'Burning Piano 2008' on YouTube: https://youtu.be/YpKT_eeCVNI

The reference to Kepler's theory in **Fairytale: The Purple Iris** comes from the Open Culture site: http://www.openculture.com/2019/05/johannes-kepler-created-a-theory-that-each-planet-sings-a-song.html. The iris in this poem and in other poems in the collection is haunted by Vahni Capildeo's irises in 'Lux Æterna et Perpetua' in *No Traveller Returns* (Salt, 2003).

The John Berger quotation in **Fairytale: The Hathersage Road** is from his recording *I Send You This Cadmium Red*, made with John Christie and Gavin Bryars (2010).

In **Fairytale: The Escapologist**, the one tree sings Patti Smith's 'Gloria', which is from her debut album *Horses* (1975). The other tree is singing Peggy Lee's title track from Nicholas Ray's *Johnny Guitar* (Republic Pictures, 1954).

A Love Supreme, in **Postcard**, is the 1965 album by John Coltrane.

Fairytale: The Vanishing Point references Paula Rego's artwork, *Little Miss Muffet*, etching and aquatint on hand-made paper (1989).

Correspondences: The Lark Ascending was written after listening to an episode of BBC Radio 4's *Tales from the Stave* with Jennifer Pike, broadcast on 2 July 2016. Also, R. Murray Schafer's 'Snow-forms' can be seen here: https://youtu.be/GiOhtgR1T0k

In **Correspondences: Song**, Etel Adnan's book is *Sea and Fog*, published by Nightboat Books (2012). The paintings of Cassandra and Helen are by Evelyn De Morgan (both 1898).

What Hendrix says to Patti Smith, in **Correspondences III**, is from her memoir, *Just Kids* (Bloomsbury, 2011). The children lost in the woods and named in song was an idea that came from a Norwegian folk tale I heard on another episode of *Tales from the Stave* in 2018: https://www.bbc.co.uk/sounds/play/b0b5t2jc. The tulips I had in mind belong to Robert Mapplethorpe (*Parrot Tulips*, 1988).

The song on the radio in **Fairytale No. 24** is 'A Rose Garden', written by Joe South in 1967 and recorded by Lynn Anderson in 1970.

Correspondences: The Rhododendron Tree. 'The Snows of Kilimanjaro' was first a story by Hemingway in 1936. The film was directed by Henry King in 1952 (Twentieth Century Fox). The Oliver Sacks references come from *The Man Who Mistook His Wife for a Hat* (Picador, 2011). And Van Morrison's 'Sweet Thing' is from *Astral Weeks* (1968). Rousseau's *Reveries of the Solitary Walker*, from 1778, are cited in Rebecca Solnit's *Wanderlust* (Granta, 2014), and the apricots quote is from *The Faraway Nearby*, also by Solnit (Granta, 2014). *Rhapsody in Blue* was composed by George Gershwin (1924), and I read about the 'Strawberry Fields Forever' editing process from Open Culture: https://www.openculture.com/2020/05/how-strawberry-fields-forever-contains-the-craziest-edit-in-beatles-history.html. The Freud references are from *The Interpretation of Dreams*, first published in 1899. Angela Pelster has a collection of essays, including 'Portrait of a Mango', called *Limber*, published by Sarabande Books in 2014. The *Nude Series* is by Georgia O'Keeffe, and I was thinking of number VIII (1917).

The woman in **Fairytale: Rain** was Chrione in Greek mythology. Her tongue was shot through by Artemis as punishment.

I wrote **Correspondences: Oak** after listening to James Canton's *The Oak Papers* (Canongate, 2020). The radio programme was Radio 4's *Book of the Week*, read by Jonathan Keeble in August 2020. The recomposer of Vivaldi was Max Richter.

Credence

Fairytale: Study for the hopeful... and **Love (Six Rituals)** are written around some of the objects and descriptions from *A History of the World in 100 Objects*, a series by Neil MacGregor, which was originally a radio production in collaboration between Radio 4 and the British Museum in 2010.

Love (Six Rituals) uses one of the Arabic stages of love models. The translations of the titles are adapted from this site: https://www.arabic-studio.com/the-11-stages-of-love-in-arabic/

The song referenced in **On Listening to *My Baby's Taking Me Home* by Sparks** is from their *Lil' Beethoven* album (2002). The Christian coins in the poem are another object from the MacGregor series, and the epigraph is from *A Celtic Miscellany* (1971), selected and translated by Kenneth Hurlstone Jackson.

The Heaney reference in **Correspondences: The Credence of Birds** is to *The Cure at Troy* (Faber, 1990). The birdsong transcriptions are from *The Wisdom of Birds: An Illustrated History of Ornithology* by Tim Birkhead (Bloomsbury, 2011). The kingfisher, pigeon and Japanese tit tricks are also adapted from Birkhead. John Cale's 'Big White Cloud' is from *Vintage Violence* (1970). The floating leaves is Henri Bergson's idea, as described by Suzanne Guerlac in *Thinking in Time: An Introduction to Henri Bergson* (Cornell University, 2006).

Reindeer references carvings from the Neil MacGregor series.

In **Postcard**, the Franz Wright epigraph, 'P.S.', is from *Walking to Martha's Vineyard* (Random House USA, 2005).

Acknowledgements

Some of these poems, or versions of poems, have appeared in the following magazines and books, to whose editors I am grateful: *Brixton Review of Books* 1; *DW Cities: Sheffield* (Dostoyevsky Wannabe); *Environs: Modern Natures* (Route 57); *The Honest Ulsterman*; *One for the Road* (smith|doorstop); *The Poetry Review*; *Wretched Strangers* (Boiler House Press).

'Correspondences: The Lark Ascending', 'On Listening to *My Baby's Taking Me Home* by Sparks' and 'Correspondences: Oak' were published in *Shearsman* 133/134 (October 2022).

'Correspondences: The Rhododendron Tree' appeared in issue 26 of *Blackbox Manifold* (Summer 2021): https://blackboxmanifold. sites.sheffield.ac.uk/issues/issues-21-28/issue-26/angelina-droza